OCEANS OF THE WORLD

THE INDIAN OCEAN

A MyReportLinks.com Book

DOREEN GONZALES

MyReportLinks.com Books

an imprint of

 Enslow Publishers, Inc.

Box 398, 40 Industrial Road
Berkeley Heights, NJ 07922
USA

MyReportLinks.com Books, an imprint of Enslow Publishers, Inc. MyReportLinks® is a registered trademark of Enslow Publishers, Inc.

Library of Congress Cataloging-in-Publication Data

Gonzales, Doreen.
    The Indian Ocean / Doreen Gonzales.
        v. cm. — (Oceans of the world)
Includes bibliographical references and index.
Contents: Report links — Indian Ocean facts — The Indian Ocean —
Resources from the Indian Ocean — The ocean floor — Life in the Indian
Ocean — Exploration — A healthy ocean.
    ISBN 0-7660-5195-1
    1. Oceanography—Indian Ocean—Juvenile literature. 2. Indian
Ocean—Juvenile literature. [1. Indian Ocean.] I. Title.
    GC721.G66 2004
    551.46'15—dc22
                                        2003016490

Printed in the United States of America

10 9 8 7 6 5 4 3 2 1

To Our Readers:
Through the purchase of this book, you and your library gain access to the Report Links that specifically back up this book.
The Publisher will provide access to the Report Links that back up this book and will keep these Report Links up to date on **www.myreportlinks.com** for three years from the book's first publication date.
We have done our best to make sure all Internet addresses in this book were active and appropriate when we went to press. However, the author and the Publisher have no control over, and assume no liability for, the material available on those Internet sites or on other Web sites they may link to.
The usage of the MyReportLinks.com Books Web site is subject to the terms and conditions stated on the Usage Policy Statement on **www.myreportlinks.com**.
A password may be required to access the Report Links that back up this book. The password is found on the bottom of page 4 of this book.
Any comments or suggestions can be sent by e-mail to comments@myreportlinks.com or to the address on the back cover.

Photo Credits: Clipart.com, pp. 33, 34, 38; © American Museum of Natural History, p. 21; © Australian Museum 2002, pp. 25, 26; © Corel Corporation, pp. 15, 23, 36; © Trident Press, p. 42; GeoAtlas, p. 10; GlobalSecurity.org, p. 17; Jose Cort/NOAA, p. 40; MarineBio.com © 1998–2004, p. 37; Mr. Ben Mieremet, Senior Advisor OSD, NOAA, p. 30; Mr. Mohammed Al Momany, Aqaba, Jordan, p. 43; MyReportLinks.com Books, p. 4; National Oceanic and Atmospheric Association (NOAA), p. 29; PBS/Nova Online, p. 19; Photos.com, pp. 1, 3, 9, 12, 13, 28.

Cover Photo: © 1997–2000 Hemera Technologies, Inc., Photos.com.

Contents

MyReportLinks.com Books
Great Books, Great Links, Great for Research!

The Report Links listed on the following four pages can save you hours of research time by **instantly** bringing you to the best Web sites relating to your report topic.

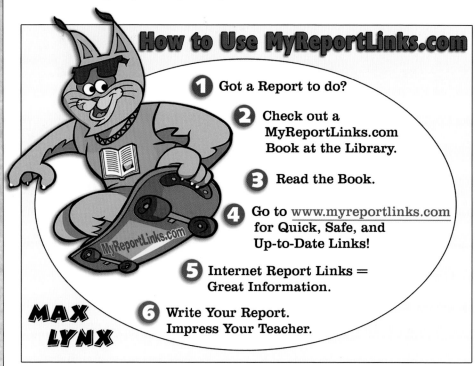

How to Use MyReportLinks.com

1 Got a Report to do?

2 Check out a MyReportLinks.com Book at the Library.

3 Read the Book.

4 Go to www.myreportlinks.com for Quick, Safe, and Up-to-Date Links!

5 Internet Report Links = Great Information.

6 Write Your Report. Impress Your Teacher.

MAX LYNX

The pre-evaluated Web sites are your links to source documents, photographs, illustrations, and maps. They also provide links to dozens—even hundreds—of Web sites about your report subject.

MyReportLinks.com Books and the MyReportLinks.com Web site save you time and make report writing easier than ever!

Please see "To Our Readers" on the copyright page for important information about this book, the MyReportLinks.com Web site, and the Report Links that back up this book. Please enter **OIN1444** if asked for a password.

Report Links

 The Internet sites described below can be accessed at http://www.myreportlinks.com

*EDITOR'S CHOICE

▶*The World Factbook*: Indian Ocean
At *The World Factbook* Web site you can learn about the Indian Ocean. Information includes geography, economy, transportation, and transnational issues.

*EDITOR'S CHOICE

▶Perry-Castañeda Library Map Collection: Indian Ocean Maps
The Perry-Castañeda Library Map Collection Web site includes many maps of the Indian Ocean, as well as maps of Madagascar, Sri Lanka, and Seychelles.

*EDITOR'S CHOICE

▶Monsoons
This site provides a brief overview of monsoons; winds that occur periodically in the Indian Ocean.

*EDITOR'S CHOICE

▶Infoplease.com: Indian Ocean
Basic information about the Indian Ocean and its characteristics can be found at the Infoplease.com Web site.

*EDITOR'S CHOICE

▶Regional Perspectives: Indian Ocean
Learn about the Indian Ocean, coral reefs, mangroves, and more.

*EDITOR'S CHOICE

▶Oceans Alive!
Oceans Alive! provides information about oceans winds, waves, and currents. Underwater exploration is another topic that is covered.

Report Links

The Internet sites described below can be accessed at http://www.myreportlinks.com

▶**Africa Environment Outlook**

The Africa Environment Outlook Web site discusses the climate of the Indian Ocean, including cyclones and other weather systems.

▶**Beyond the Reef**

The Beyond the Reef Web site provides basic information about plankton, phytoplankton, zooplankton, and more.

▶**Blue Planet Challenge**

At the Blue Planet Challenge Web site you can explore oceans and ocean life. Facts about the oceans, including the Indian Ocean, are provided.

▶**Cetacean Information**

The Whale Songs Web site contains descriptions of ocean dwellers such as whales, dolphins, and porpoises.

▶**Discover Our Earth**

At the Discover Our Earth Web site you will learn about continental drift, seafloor spreading, and much more.

▶**Honolulu Zoo: Angonoka Tortoise**

On this site from the Honolulu Zoo you will find information on the angonoka tortoise. The angonoka is found on the island of Madagascar and is one of the most endangered tortoises in the world.

▶**Lonely Planet: Maldives**

The Maldives is a nation of islands in the Indian Ocean. Read about this country's history and culture at the Lonely Planet Web site.

▶**Mangroves: Arabian Sea Forests**

The Arabian Wildlife Web site informs people about mangrove trees and swamps along the Arabian coast.

Any comments? Contact us: **comments@myreportlinks.com**

Report Links

▶**Marine Biology**

At the Marinebio.com Web site users may learn many interesting facts about phytoplankton, ocean mysteries, and scuba diving.

▶**Milstein Hall of Ocean Life**

Learn all about the world's largest mammal, the blue whale, at the Milstein Hall of Ocean Life.

▶**National Ocean Service**

Find out about oceans, coral reefs, and much more at the National Ocean Service Web site.

▶**Ocean Explorer**

This well-researched Web site covers ocean exploration, technology, projects, and history.

▶**Ocean Planet**

Ocean Planet, a Smithsonian Web site, provides a tour of their exhibit about the ocean. You can learn about ocean science, sea people, and much more.

▶**Oceans Alive**

The Oceans Alive Web site provides research about whales, sea grass, seamounts, and much more.

▶**Reef Education Network**

The Reef Education Network is a great place to learn about coral reefs. Information includes how old they are, how many types there are, and much more.

▶**Saving the Magpie Robin**

Learn about the magpie robin and how efforts to save the magpie have increased its population.

The Internet sites described below can be accessed at http://www.myreportlinks.com

▶**Seychelles: A Country Study**

The Library of Congress Web site provides a concise overview of Seychelles, a nation of islands in the Indian Ocean.

▶**Sri Lanka: A Country Study**

Take a look at a concise profile of Sri Lanka at the Library of Congress Web site. Research its people, history, and much more.

▶**The Voyage of the Odyssey**

Find out about the island nation of Sri Lanka. Click on "Track the Voyage" to learn more about traveling on the Indian Ocean.

▶**Where in the World Is Diego Garcia?**

Infoplease.com provides a brief description of the island of Diego Garcia. See where it is located and what it is used for.

▶**Wild Indonesia**

Indonesia and the island of Anak Krakatau are profiled at this PBS Web site.

▶*The World Factbook*: **Madagascar**

The World Factbook Web site holds information about the island of Madagascar, including its geography, people, and government.

▶*The World Factbook*: **Pacific Ocean**

The World Factbook Web site provides information about the Pacific Ocean, including its geography, economy, transportation, and transnational issues that affect this ocean that neighbors the Indian Ocean to the east.

▶*The World Factbook*: **Southern Ocean**

The World Factbook Web site provides information about the Southern Ocean, which borders the Indian Ocean to the south. Geography, economy, transportation, and transnational issues are some of the topics covered.

Indian Ocean Facts

▶ **Area***

About 26,469,600 square
miles
About 68,556,000 square
kilometers

▶ **Average Depth**

13,002 feet
3,963 meters

▶ **Greatest Known Depth**

The Sunda Trench in
Indonesia
24,442 feet
7,450 meters

▶ **Greatest Distances**

North to South is about
6,140 miles (9,880
kilometers).
East to West is about 6,200
miles (10,000 kilometers).

▶ **Surface Temperature**

Highest—about 90°F
(32°C) in the Persian
Gulf and Red Sea.
Lowest—below 30°F
(⁻1°C) near Antarctic
waters.

All metric and Celsius measurements used in this book are estimates.

▲ A boat floats at sea around the Seychelles Islands in the Indian Ocean.

A GIANT 'M'

The Indian Ocean lies between Africa on the west and Australia and Indonesia on the east. Asia is the ocean's northern boundary. The Southern Ocean borders it to the south.[1]

Most of the Indian Ocean lies in the Southern Hemisphere. The outline of the ocean forms a giant 'M' on the surface of the globe.

The Indian Ocean covers over 26 million square miles (68 million square kilometers).[2] It is the third largest ocean

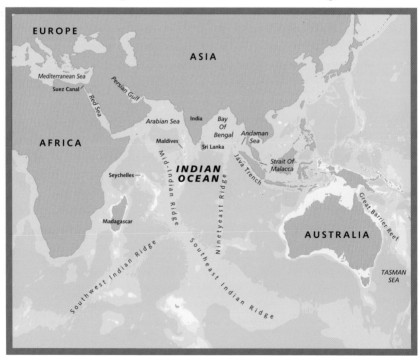

▲ *A world map of the Indian Ocean.*

on Earth. The land of the continental United States could fit in the Indian Ocean more than five times.[3]

The Indian Ocean holds several seas. *Sea* can be another word for ocean. It can also mean a part of an ocean. The Arabian Sea and the Andaman Sea are both a part of the Indian Ocean. So is the long, narrow Red Sea that separates Africa from Asia. The Persian Gulf and the Bay of Bengal are other large bodies of water that make up the Indian Ocean.

The Indian Ocean is also full of islands. Many are part of the island country of Indonesia. The Maldives and Sri Lanka are other islands located in the ocean. Madagascar is the largest Indian Ocean island. It lies east of the southeastern tip of Africa.

▶ Climate

Much of the Indian Ocean lies within the tropics. The tropics are the areas 1,600 miles (2,575 kilometers) on either side of the equator. The tropics have warm to hot temperatures all year long. The air above the tropical Indian Ocean ranges from about 60° to 85°F (15° to 29°C).

The waters of the tropical ocean stay warm, too. Surface water rarely drops below 70°F (21°C). In July, the temperature of the water can reach up 90°F (32°C).

The air is much cooler south of the tropics. In the winter, it dips to around 40°F (4°C). The water here is colder, too.

Indian Ocean water also gets colder as it gets deeper because of the lack of sunlight toward the bottom of the ocean. Water in the deepest part of the ocean is near freezing.

An aerial photo of the island of Madagascar. Off the east coast of Africa, Madagascar is the largest island in the Indian Ocean.

▶ Winds

There are three major wind systems in the Indian Ocean. The first is the monsoon. A monsoon is a wind that changes direction with the season. From November to March, winds that begin in central Asia blow southwesterly across the Indian Ocean. This wind is called the northeast monsoon. In April, the monsoon shifts. Now the southwest monsoon blows. Its winds begin over the Indian Ocean. They blow northeasterly across the water and then onto land. This monsoon is called the wet monsoon. It brings heavy rains to Asia.

People in India, Bangladesh, and Thailand depend on the monsoon rains. These rains are the source of their drinking water. They also use it to water crops. Yet monsoon rains can also be destructive. They sometimes start floods that ruin property and even cause death.

The second Indian Ocean wind system is the trade winds. Trade winds begin in the Southern Hemisphere and blow toward the equator.

The last kind of wind is the prevailing westerly winds. They move from west to east.

Cyclones

Sometimes winds develop into cyclones. A cyclone is a severe storm with whirling winds. Cyclones are common in the tropical areas of the Indian Ocean. They form at sea, then move westerly. At times they strike land. Like monsoons, a cyclone can cause property damage and kill people.

Currents

Indian Ocean winds create currents, too. A current is water that moves in a constant and regular motion. It is like a river in the sea.

▲ *Winds and currents make it possible to enjoy sailing. This yacht is sailing off the coast of the Seychelles Islands.*

One Indian Ocean current flows westward along the equator. When it reaches Africa, it flows south. It then turns and flows east to Australia. This current is known as the south equatorial current.

The direction of currents north the equator is determined by which monsoon is blowing. They flow either east or west depending on the season.

▶ Tides

The Indian Ocean also moves in tides. A tide is the level at which water hits the shore.

Tides are caused by the Moon's gravity. When the Moon is on one side of Earth, its gravity pulls on the water it faces. This makes each wave go a little higher onto the land. As Earth rotates, the Moon pulls on different waters. The water that was high recedes. Now, water in another part of the ocean is drawn farther up the shore. This lasts until Earth and the Moon change position again. At any one place, tides change twice each day.

RESOURCES FROM THE INDIAN OCEAN

The Indian Ocean provides humans with many types of resources. These include fish to eat and fuels such as oil and natural gas to burn. The Indian Ocean also acts as a trade route over which goods are shipped from and to many lands. Many people also use the Indian Ocean for recreational activities such as swimming and boating.

▶ Oil

Areas below the Indian Ocean are rich in oil and natural gas. Oil and gas lie in deposits beneath the seabed. Huge

▲ These supertankers are loading oil in the Persian Gulf, off the coast of Saudi Arabia. The Gulf region is the largest oil-producing area in the world.

drills and pumps are needed to pull them to the surface. These are built on platforms called offshore wells.

Forty percent of the world's offshore oil comes from the Indian Ocean.[1] There are wells near India, Australia, and Africa.

The majority of Indian Ocean oil, however, comes from below the Persian Gulf. The countries around the gulf are rich in oil, too. The land and sea make this area the largest oil-producing region on Earth.[2] In fact, more than one fourth of all the oil in the world comes from Persian Gulf countries.[3]

The United States uses more than 2 million barrels of Persian Gulf oil each day. This is about one fourth of all the oil the United States imports. Countries in Western Europe import half of their oil from the Persian Gulf. In addition, nearly 75 percent of all the oil Japan uses comes from this area.[4]

▶ Trade Routes

Most Persian Gulf oil gets to other countries by way of the Indian Ocean. This makes the ocean one of the most important transportation systems in the world.

Many oil tankers sail around Africa to Atlantic Ocean ports. Others travel to Pacific Ocean ports through the Strait of Malacca. This is a channel between the Malay Peninsula and the island of Sumatra.

One of the most popular trade routes is through the Suez Canal. The Suez Canal is a man-made waterway. It connects the Red Sea to the Mediterranean Sea. The canal is the most direct route from the Indian Ocean to many ports in Europe.

In addition to oil, other goods are shipped across the Indian. The most common are iron, coal, rubber, and tea.

Ships also bring goods to cities around the Indian Ocean. Bombay (India), Yangon (Myanmar), Perth (Australia), and Dar es Salaam (Tanzania) are a few of the ocean's major ports.

Military Bases

Some countries have military bases on the Indian Ocean. The United States has one on an island named Diego Garcia, which is near the middle of the ocean. The base there has airstrips for fighter and cargo planes, and harbors for warships and submarines.

Manganese Nodules

Another natural resource that comes from the Indian Ocean is manganese nodules. These are rocks about the size of potatoes. Thousands of them are scattered across the bottom of the ocean. Manganese is used to refine and

▲ The United States maintains a military base on the island of Diego Garcia in the Indian Ocean. This jet is about ready for takeoff from the base.

strengthen steel. All steel contains at least some manganese. Manganese dioxide is used to make many things such as batteries, paints, dyes, and is also used to develop photos.

Although these nodules, or rocks, are mostly made of manganese, they also contain copper, nickel, and cobalt. It is expensive to gather these nodules. Therefore, few are mined.

Fish

The Indian Ocean is an important source of food for the people who live near it. Most fishing is done on small boats. The catch is eaten by fishers' families or sold in local markets.

There are a few large fishing ships that operate in the Indian Ocean. They catch mainly shrimp and tuna.[5]

Nature's Museum

A number of the earth's most unique animals inhabit islands located in the Indian Ocean. Twelve species of birds seen nowhere else in the world live on the islands of Seychelles. Among them are the magpie robin and the black parrot.

Another rare species is the angonoka tortoise. It lives on Madagascar. The angonoka grows to 18 inches (46 centimeters) long. There were only about four hundred angonokas alive at the beginning of 2003.[6]

Tourism

Unusual wildlife, a warm climate, and sandy beaches make the tropical islands of the Indian Ocean, such as Mauritius and Seychelles, popular vacation spots. The tourism industry is important to the people who live near the ocean. Vacation resorts, shops, and restaurants provide

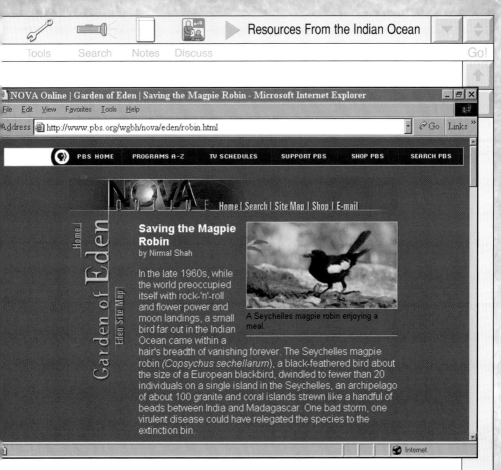

NOVA Online | Garden of Eden | Saving the Magpie Robin - Microsoft Internet Explorer

File Edit View Favorites Tools Help

Address http://www.pbs.org/wgbh/nova/eden/robin.html   Go   Links

PBS HOME   PROGRAMS A-Z   TV SCHEDULES   SUPPORT PBS   SHOP PBS   SEARCH PBS

NOVA   Home | Search | Site Map | Shop | E-mail

Saving the Magpie Robin
by Nirmal Shah

In the late 1960s, while the world preoccupied itself with rock-'n'-roll and flower power and moon landings, a small bird far out in the Indian Ocean came within a

A Seychelles magpie robin enjoying a meal.

hair's breadth of vanishing forever. The Seychelles magpie robin (*Copsychus sechellarum*), a black-feathered bird about the size of a European blackbird, dwindled to fewer than 20 individuals on a single island in the Seychelles, an archipelago of about 100 granite and coral islands strewn like a handful of beads between India and Madagascar. One bad storm, one virulent disease could have relegated the species to the extinction bin.

Internet

The Seychelles Islands have twelve species of birds found nowhere else in the world. The magpie robin, shown here, is one of those species.

jobs for many island inhabitants. Without tourists, these people might have no work.

Water Cycle

People everywhere depend on the Indian Ocean in one very basic way. It helps keep the earth supplied with water. Ocean water evaporates, then condenses to form clouds. When the clouds become heavy with condensation, the moisture falls to the ground as rain or snow.

Some of this precipitation is used. Much ends up back in the ocean to continue the cycle. All of the earth's oceans are needed to keep the water cycle alive.

Chapter 3

THE OCEAN FLOOR

The floor of the Indian Ocean is home to many interesting plants and sea animals. Mountains and volcanoes are among the fascinating things that line the ocean floor.

▷ Continental Shelf

The bottom of the Indian Ocean slopes gently from the shore toward the deep ocean. This gradual incline is called the continental shelf. Most of the Indian Ocean's continental shelf is about 75 miles (121 kilometers) long. Between Australia and New Guinea, though, the shelf extends 600 miles (966 kilometers).

The ocean bottom drops sharply at the end of the continental shelf. This steep cliff is the continental slope. The floor of the deep sea lies at the bottom of the slope.

Several large basins line the Indian Ocean floor. A basin is a flat area covered with a thick layer of sand. The average depth of the Indian Ocean is about 13,002 feet (3,963 meters).[1] Yet the entire seafloor is not smooth. It has many features.

▷ Java Trench

Deep channels cut through Indian Ocean basins. These narrow gashes are called trenches. The longest trench in the Indian Ocean is Java Trench. It runs for nearly 1,600 miles (2,575 kilometers) along the western coast of Indonesia.

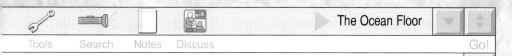

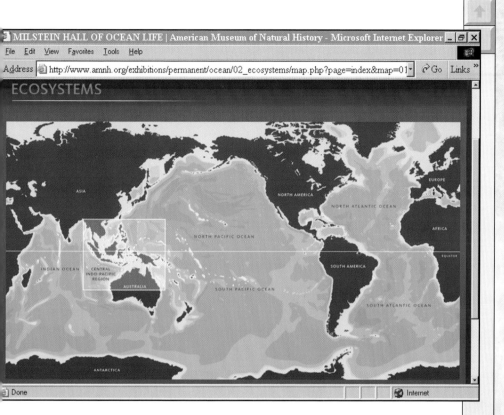

ECOSYSTEMS

ASIA

NORTH AMERICA

EUROPE

NORTH ATLANTIC OCEAN

AFRICA

NORTH PACIFIC OCEAN

EQUATOR

INDIAN OCEAN

CENTRAL
INDO-PACIFIC
REGION

AUSTRALIA

SOUTH AMERICA

SOUTH PACIFIC OCEAN

SOUTH ATLANTIC OCEAN

ANTARCTICA

△ The floor of the Indian Ocean has many features. Among them are the coral reefs located off the coast of Australia.

The deepest point in the Indian Ocean is in Java Trench. It lies 24,442 feet (7,450 meters) below the surface of the sea.[2] This point is called the Sunda Trench.

Seamounts

Seamounts are another interesting feature of the Indian Ocean floor. Seamounts are cone-shaped mountains with flat tops. Some rise 3,300 feet (1,006 meters) from the ocean bottom. Many seamounts are found in the waters northeast of Madagascar.

Mountains

Mountain ranges also run along the ocean bottom. One range is called the Ninetyeast Ridge. It runs from north to south on the eastern side of the ocean.

Another set of ranges forms an upside-down 'Y' on the ocean floor. The 'Y' begins in the Arabian Sea. Near the middle of the ocean, the range branches two ways. The Southwest Indian Ridge runs to the southwest. The other range branches southeastward. It is called the Southeast Indian Ridge.

The Y-shaped ridge is part of a longer mountain range called the mid-ocean ridge. The mid-ocean ridge runs through every ocean in the world. It is important in a geological theory called plate tectonics. According to plate tectonics, the earth's crust sits on several huge pieces of rock, or plates. The mid-ocean ridge runs along the edges of some plates. Powerful forces inside the earth push the plates together and pull them apart.

Seafloor Spreading and Subduction

Plate movement can create cracks in the earth's crust. Molten rock from inside the earth rises to fill the cracks. When it cools, it becomes new seafloor. This process is called seafloor spreading.

Indian Ocean ridges spread about two inches (five centimeters) a year.[3] Yet even though the seafloor is spreading, the Indian Ocean is not getting bigger. This is because old seafloor is constantly disappearing. This happens at a place called a subduction zone.

Subduction zones are areas where seafloor is pushed under the earth's crust. There it falls into the deep earth

▲ *This whitetip reef shark is looking for food at the bottom of the Red Sea, one of the seas that are part of the Indian Ocean.*

and becomes molten rock. Java Trench is the main subduction zone in the Indian Ocean.

Earthquakes and Volcanoes

All of the pushing and pulling of plates causes ocean earthquakes and volcanoes. Most occur along mid-ocean ridges and subduction zones. Much of the time they are not felt on land. Sometimes, though, they trigger huge waves that reach land and cause destruction.

This happened in 1883 on an uninhabited island called Krakatau. That year, a huge volcanic explosion erupted. It threw rocks fifty miles into the air. The volcano destroyed most of the island. It set off a huge wave. The wave flooded nearby islands and killed thirty-six thousand people.[4]

Chapter 4

LIFE IN THE INDIAN OCEAN

A wide variety of animal and plant life populates the Indian Ocean. Some species are used for food and medicine, while others are simply interesting creatures that make the ocean's ecosystem unique.

▷ The Ocean Ecosystem

Each organism depends on several others to survive. This is called an ecosystem. The Indian Ocean ecosystem includes the largest animals on Earth. It also includes life so small it can only be seen with a microscope.

Many animals of the sea cannot swim. Instead, they float about with the ocean's waves and currents. These animals are called zooplankton. Most zooplankton are tiny, but some grow quite large.

The ocean also contains microscopic plants that float in its waters, called phytoplankton. Phytoplankton and zooplankton make up the plankton.

The plankton is vital to the ocean's ecosystem. Without it, no sea creature would survive. It is the food of small ocean animals. These small ocean animals that eat the plankton become food for larger ones. These larger ocean animals are then eaten by even larger ones. This chain continues to the biggest animals of the ocean. Therefore, all sea life needs plankton.

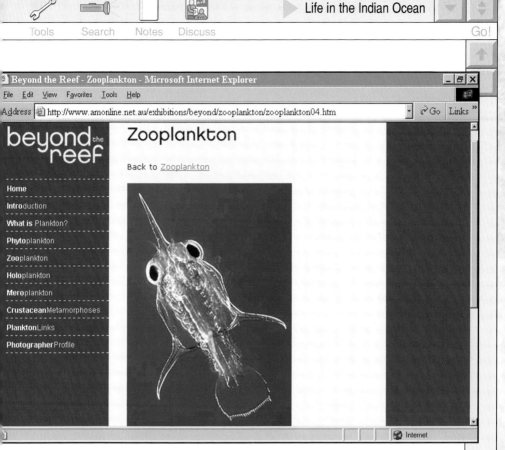

Tools   Search   Notes   Discuss   Go!

Beyond the Reef - Zooplankton - Microsoft Internet Explorer

File   Edit   View   Favorites   Tools   Help

Address   http://www.amonline.net.au/exhibitions/beyond/zooplankton/zooplankton04.htm   Go   Links

beyondthe**reef**

Zooplankton

Back to Zooplankton

Home

Introduction

What is Plankton?

Phytoplankton

Zooplankton

Holoplankton

Meroplankton

CrustaceanMetamorphoses

PlanktonLinks

PhotographerProfile

Internet

▲ Zooplankton are animals that do not swim, but instead float along with the ocean's waves and currents. Most of them are too small to be seen by the human eye.

▶ Whales

Actually, there are some very large animals that survive solely by eating plankton. These animals are called the baleen whales.

Baleen whales have thin plates of a bone-like substance inside their mouths. This is called baleen. It is covered with brushlike fibers. Baleen whales eat by taking in great gulps of water. They push the water out of their mouths, trapping plankton in the baleen. The whales then swallow the plankton.

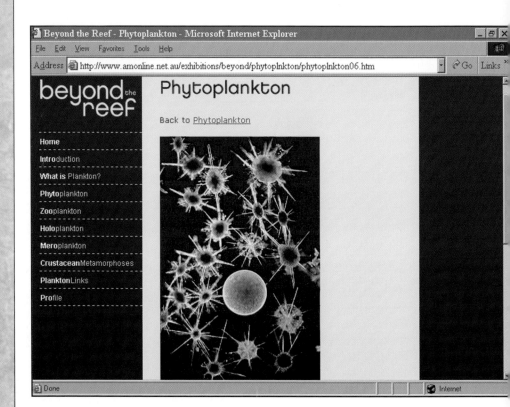

Phytoplankton are plants that float in the ocean. Seaweed is a type of phytoplankton.

Fin, sei, and blue whales are all baleen whales. They are found in the Indian Ocean. The blue whale is the largest animal on Earth. It can grow to 100 feet (30 meters) long and weigh 220 tons (200 metric tons). Its favorite food is a kind of zooplankton called krill. An adult blue whale's stomach can hold 2 tons (1.8 metric tons) of krill.[1]

Toothed whales also live in the Indian Ocean. They are referred to as "toothed" because unlike the baleen whales they have teeth and eat fish. One of them, the sperm whale, prefers tropical waters.

Several Indian Ocean whales travel from place to place. They live in the far south during the winter months. Each spring they swim north to warmer waters. There the females give birth. This movement is called migration.

The smallest whales of the Indian Ocean are the dolphins and porpoises. Their favorite foods are squid and fish.

Squid and Octopus

Many different kinds of squid live in the Indian Ocean. They can vary in size from one to forty feet (0.3 to 12 meters) long. Squid have ten tentacles. Each tentacle is lined with sucking disks. The squid use these disks to capture prey.

Octopuses live in the Indian Ocean, too. They are related to the squid but have only eight arms. The smallest species of octopus is found in the Indian Ocean. It is only an inch (2.5 centimeters) long. Called the Octopus wolfi, this creature weighs less than one ounce (28 grams).

Fish

The largest fish in the Indian Ocean are the tuna, swordfish, sailfish, and shark. All of these fish like warm tropical waters. They are strong, fast swimmers. This makes them expert predators.

Sharks may be the most well-known predators of the sea. Several different kinds live in the Indian Ocean. The smallest is only about as long as a pencil. The largest is the whale shark. It can grow to be fifty feet (fifteen meters) long.

One of the most dangerous sharks is the great white. It can grow up to twenty feet (six meters) in length. Although they prefer a diet of marine animals, great whites have been known to attack people on rare occasions.[2]

Several species of smaller fish swim the Indian Ocean. Among them are flying fish, mackerel, and sardine.

▲ *Sardines are just one of many species of small fish that swim in the waters of the Indian Ocean.*

▷ Bottom Dwellers

Some animals stay on the bottom of the ocean. Many eat particles of decaying plants and animals that float down from above. Several, like the clam and sponge, filter food particles out of the water. Some, such as the snail and sea cucumber, scrape or grind food from the rocks and mud on the ocean floor.

Other bottom dwellers trick prey into their mouths. Many have light organs that blink on and off to attract prey. Others have huge mouths that animals swim into without even knowing it.

▷ Birds

Several bird species depend on Indian Ocean animals as a source of food. Terns, noddies, and black frigates live in the tropical areas. Petrels and albatross live in Indian Ocean regions farther south.

All of these birds spend their days at sea looking for food. Many nest on land at night. Some seabirds actually live at sea. They come to land only once a year to lay eggs and raise babies.

Marine Turtles

Marine turtles spend most of their time at sea, too. Like many seabirds, they only come to land to lay eggs and raise their young.

Green turtles are numerous in the Indian Ocean. They sometimes swim thousands of miles to nest where they hatched.[3] They can grow up to 650 pounds (295 kilograms). Green turtles eat ocean plants.

▲ *There are many sea turtles in the Indian Ocean.*

Dugongs

Another plant eater is the dugong. These mammals live in warm, coastal waters. They can grow to be 10 feet (3 meters) long and weigh 650 pounds (295 kilograms). Dugongs have blunt snouts with bristly whiskers. The males have two upper tusks.

The dugongs move about in small groups. They eat sea grass by pushing it into their mouths with their flippers.

Plants

Sea grass is an ocean plant with roots that grow into the muddy seafloor. Great amounts grow in warm water areas. Sea grass beds are like meadows in the ocean.

Other large plants grow in the Indian Ocean, too. They are called seaweed. Some seaweeds attach themselves to rocks and mud. Others float, and are part of the plankton. Seaweeds can be brown, green, or red.

▲ A mangrove tree surrounded by coral rock. Mangrove trees grow in warm, muddy water along some Indian Ocean coasts.

All ocean plants need sunlight to make food. Therefore, plants can only grow in the top layer of water where the sunlight penetrates.

Mangroves

Another common plant of the Indian Ocean is the mangrove tree. Mangroves grow in muddy seawater near warm coasts. Their roots grow up and out of the mud.

Mangroves grow in groups. Their roots twist and weave around each other like a tangled mass of rope. Groups of mangroves create a habitat known as a mangrove swamp. Mangrove swamps thrive around northern Australia, Africa, India, Indonesia, and Southeast Asia. These swamps have a unique ecosystem. It is filled with birds, crabs, and fish.

One of the strangest fish of the mangrove swamp is the mudskipper fish. The mudskipper uses its fins to crawl out of the ocean and scoot across the muddy shore. It even climbs up mangrove roots and onto tree branches. Mudskippers can stay out of the water for long periods of time.

Saltwater crocodiles also inhabit mangrove swamps. These are the biggest crocodiles in the world. They can weigh over a ton. This is almost as much as a small car.

Coral

Another sub-ecosystem of the Indian Ocean is built around the polyp. Polyps are animals that take calcium out of the seawater. They use it to make their own skeletons. When a polyp dies, its body decays, but the skeleton remains.

Polyps are only an inch long. However, they attach themselves to one another to build large structures. This is called coral. At times coral grows so big it makes reefs

or ridges under the sea. Coral reefs grow in warm, clear, shallow waters.

The tropical Indian Ocean is filled with coral reefs. Many are found along the southern coasts of Bangladesh, Burma, and India. There are also reefs along the eastern coast of Africa.

Coral grows in a wide variety of amazing shapes and brilliant colors. It can be shaped like domes, baskets, feathery fans, and fingers. Coral ranges in color from red, to yellow, to orange, to purple.

Hundreds of different kinds of fish live around Indian Ocean reefs. The tang, angelfish, butterfly fish, and sea-horse are just a few. Most are brightly colored. Many are decorated with stripes, spots, or speckles. These markings help them blend into their surroundings.

Several other marine animals live in coral reefs as well. Sponges, worms, crabs, clams, sea urchins, and starfish are common there. In fact, reefs are sometimes called the rain-forests of the sea. This is because they are home to so many different species of life.

EXPLORATION

The Indian Ocean was the first ocean to be used as a trade route.[1] People have been sailing on it for at least three thousand years. Most of them stayed close to shore.

Arab sailors traded along the East African coast beginning around A.D. 500. They used wooden boats with triangle-shaped sails called dhows. People still travel the Indian Ocean in dhows today. These early Arabs used the monsoons and trade winds to help them travel.[2]

Ancient Chinese traders also sailed the Indian. By the early 1400s, people from China, India, and Africa were making frequent voyages on the Indian Ocean.

▶ Explorers From Europe

In 1497, Vasco da Gama left Portugal with four ships and 170 men. He sailed around Africa and up its eastern coast. There, da Gama hired

Sailing for the country of ▶ Portugal, Italian explorer Vasco da Gama sailed around the southern tip of Africa and into the Indian Ocean.

▲ *In 1872, the H.M.S.* Challenger *set sail from Great Britain on a quest to explore the world's oceans. The ship and its crew spent six months researching the Indian Ocean.*

an Arab pilot named Ahmad Ibn Majid. The pilot guided him across the ocean to India.

Da Gama returned to Portugal in 1499. Only fifty-five men survived the entire trip. Along the way, his expedition opened the first all-water trade route from Europe to Asia. Sailors from Holland, England, and France were soon sailing to the Indian Ocean and beyond.

In 1521, Juan Sebastián de Elcano crossed the central part of the ocean. De Elcano was from Spain. Later, from 1642 until 1644, Dutchman Abel Tasman explored the waters around Australia. He discovered an Indian Ocean island, now called Tasmania after him. Then, in 1772, Captain James Cook of Great Britain explored the southern reaches of the Indian. Cook and his crew learned much about the ocean's size.

Exploring For Science

The H.M.S. *Challenger,* captained by Sir George Strong Nares, was the first vessel to take a voyage simply for science. Its crew was on an oceanographic mission. Oceanography is the study of the ocean and its environment.

The *Challenger* left Great Britain in 1872. It traveled many oceans, spending six months on the Indian Ocean. The scientists on board wanted to know more about what lie below the sea. For example, they were trying to answer such questions as, "How deep was the ocean? What was the water like at different depths? What kinds of plants and animals lived in the sea?" Among other things, they were able to calculate the ocean's temperature, the depths of the basins, and charted and surveyed much of the ocean. The results of the findings made by the ship's crew were published in fifty volumes over the course of fifteen years.

Twentieth-Century Research

From 1940 until 1960, many ships sailed the Indian Ocean on oceanographic expeditions. One was named *Challenger II* after the famous research ship of the 1800s.

The *Challenger II* measured ocean depth using an echo sounder. This device shot sound waves at the ocean bottom. Scientists then measured how long it took for the sound to return to the surface. They used this number to figure out the depth of the seafloor.

The International Indian Ocean Expedition began in 1960.[3] For five years, scientists from many nations worked together on several research ships. They learned much about the ocean.

▷ The Deep Sea Drilling Project

In 1968, the Deep Sea Drilling Project began. Scientists drilled about six hundred holes in the world's oceans, including the Indian. Pipes were thrust deep into the seabed. Each one pulled up a long tube of sediment. The pipes were carefully opened and emptied. The insides are called core samples.

Scientists studied the core samples. They found several different layers in each one. Some layers were made of clay, others sandstone. Some contained fossils. Scientists even found grains of pollen in some.

Experts used special equipment to determine the age of different layers. This provided them with clues about the geological history of the earth. The oldest seafloor they found was 175 million years old. It is located along the east coast of Africa, from Somalia to South Africa.

▲ The blue-spotted stingray is among the interesting and exotic species of fish that swim along the floor of the Indian Ocean.

Animal cams are used to study many forms of ocean life in the Indian Ocean. The Galapagos shark is just one species that marine biologists research.

One of the experts' most important findings was that the seafloor was spreading.[4] This gave support to the plate tectonics theory.

More than two thousand holes have been drilled since the Deep Sea Drilling Project began. Samples from them are stored in a core library.[5] This allows scientists to continue their studies by having ready access to these samples.

Research Today

The Deep Sea Drilling Project was replaced by a new project, which is still active. Two new ships were launched

▲ *The sun sets over the Indian Ocean. This view is from the island of Bali, Indonesia.*

in 2003. One can drill twenty-three thousand feet (seven thousand meters) into the seafloor.[6]

There are other studies being done on the Indian Ocean, too. Some oceanographers are researching the ocean's monsoons and currents. Their work could improve weather forecasts. It might help scientists predict changes in the climate.

Marine biologists are studying Indian Ocean life. Many are interested in the unique species of the Indian. One of their most useful tools is the animal cam. This is a tiny camera that is carefully attached to marine animals. When the animals are released, biologists can monitor their movements and actions.[7]

Scientists have learned a great deal about the Indian Ocean since humans first sailed its waters. Yet there is still much to learn.

Chapter 6

A HEALTHY OCEAN

In many places the Indian Ocean is the cleanest ocean on Earth. However, some areas are heavily polluted. The Persian Gulf, for example, has the most polluted water in the world. The main pollutant is oil. It is so severe, oil can be seen in the water from outer space.[1]

▶ Oil Pollution

Oil pollution in the Indian Ocean comes mainly from spills on land. It runs to rivers that flow into the sea. Oil is also leaked from ships and oil platforms.

The largest Indian Ocean oil spill, however, was not an accident. In 1991, the ruler of Iraq, Saddam Hussein, dumped 460 million gallons of oil into the Persian Gulf. He wanted to punish the United States and other Western countries that had defeated him in the Persian Gulf War. By wasting the oil, he thought he would force these nations to have to spend a lot more to get their oil.[2]

The oil spill caused severe damage. Thousands of animals were killed immediately. More died later from being coated with oil. Few plants and animals lived in the polluted areas a year after the spill.[3]

▶ Poisons in the Sea

Chemicals also pollute the Indian Ocean. Factories on land sometimes dump chemical waste into rivers that run to the ocean.

▲ This fishing workboat has just finished surrounding a school of tuna in the western part of the Indian Ocean. Water pollution threatens the quality of fish in the ocean, and could put the people that eat the fish in danger of becoming ill.

More chemical pollution comes from farmers. Pesticides are used to kill insects that eat crops. Rains often wash these chemicals into the Indian.

Human sewage is another problem. It is often dumped into the sea.

Toxic substances can kill marine plants and animals immediately. Even small amounts are harmful to marine life. Fish that survive pollution are not always safe to eat. Furthermore, it only takes a little pollution to kill plankton. This disrupts food chains, which changes entire ecosystems.

▶ The Ocean As a Garbage Dump

Another pollutant is ordinary garbage that people throw into the sea. All types of garbage can make it into the earth's oceans, but some types of trash are more dangerous to the marine life than others. Dolphins, fish, and sea turtles sometimes mistake plastic bags for squid. Swallowed plastic can be deadly.

Marine animals also die when they get caught in plastic collars from six-pack beverage cans. Some are killed when they become tangled in old, unused fishing nets.

▶ Endangered Coral Reefs

Coral reefs are popular tourist attractions. People visit the reefs to snorkel or scuba dive. Yet too many divers in one area can "trample" a reef. Their boats often damage the coral. Furthermore, hundreds of tons of shells and coral are taken from reefs each year as novelties. Too much fishing also endangers reefs. Fish are caught for food or sold for aquariums.

Some fishers use illegal fishing methods to increase their catch. One method uses cyanide to poison fish. Cyanide paralyzes fish for a short time so they can be caught. These fish recover, but other nearby animals are often killed.[4]

Another illegal practice is dynamiting coral. Fish that are killed by the explosion are harvested. This method destroys coral that has been growing for hundreds of years. In addition, it kills creatures the fishers do not want.

▶ Endangered Mangrove Swamps

Some of the world's largest cities are on or near the Indian Ocean.[5] Many are growing. This creates a need for more

| Mangroves: Arabian sea Forests - Microsoft Internet Explorer |
| File   Edit   View   Favorites   Tools   Help |
| Address   http://www.arabianwildlife.com/current/mangrove.html   Go   Links |

Arabian WILDLIFE

MANGROVES: ARABIAN SEA FORESTS

- HOMEPAGE
- CURRENT ISSUE
- ISSUE ARCHIVE
- ANIMALS
- PLANTS
- NATURAL EMIRATES
- NEWS
- SEARCH
- LINKS
- BOOKS
- WEB BOARDS
- CONTACT US
- SUBSCRIBE

By Rob Baldwin

The largest areas of mangrove in the Gulf area occur along the coast of Iran, with an estimated 9000 hectares (ha) of mangrove. It is estimated that a further 3500-4000 ha remains along the Arabian Gulf coasts of Saudi Arabia, Bahrain and UAE. This figure is declining all the time, as rapid development threatens increasingly isolated mangroves stands. Along the Oman coast, just over 1000 ha of mangrove remain, including the Khor Kalba stand, which straddles the Oman/UAE border. There are few remaining mangrove stands on the Yemen coast of the Arabian Sea and the entire eastern shoreline of the Arabian region therefore hosts very restricted mangrove habitats.

The small mangrove stand at Khor Liwa is situated on the Batinah coast of Oman, approximately 45 kilometres southeast

Done   Internet

Some mangrove swamps are cut and used for lumber and firewood. This destroys the ecosystem and threatens the way of life of other animals and fish that live there.

houses, stores, and schools. Many are built near Indian Ocean coasts. Sometimes mangrove swamps are cut down to make room for new buildings. Mangrove trees are also cut for lumber and firewood.

Cutting mangrove swamps leads to floods. In addition, it destroys the mangrove ecosystem. Experts say that one half of India's mangrove swamps have already been lost.[6]

Loss of ecosystems results in loss of species. Without a place to live, an animal population decreases. When a species' numbers drop very low, it is said to be endangered. This means the animal could become extinct.

Endangered Species

Several species of the Indian Ocean are endangered. For example, most large whales like the blue whale are endangered. This is mainly because they have been overhunted.

Hunting has endangered turtles, too. The green turtle is hunted for food. The hawksbill is hunted for its shell, which is then made into ornaments and jewelry.

The dugong is another endangered species. Dugongs have been hunted for their hides and meat. Furthermore, development has ruined many of the sea grass beds they need to survive.

Other Indian Ocean animals that are endangered or at risk of becoming endangered include sharks, seahorses, and swordfish.[7]

Protecting Species

Many people and organizations are working to protect endangered animals. Some countries with Indian Ocean coasts

As of 2004, seahorses were not officially on the endangered list, but many groups are closely monitoring the declining numbers of the species.

have created sea sanctuaries or marine reserves. These are places where marine life cannot be disturbed.

Furthermore, international laws prohibit hunting endangered species anywhere in the ocean. People hope that by protecting endangered species their numbers will recover. If not, they could suffer the same fate as the dodo bird.

Large numbers of the dodo bird once lived on an Indian Ocean island. During the 1600s, sailors who stopped on the island killed dodos for food. The birds were easy prey because they could not fly. The sailors eventually killed so many, the dodo became extinct.

Seventeenth-century sailors did not know their actions could wipe out an entire species. They did not know this would harm other species of the ecosystem. These ancient seafarers had no idea they were changing the earth forever.

People of recent eras have known this. It is up to the leaders and citizens of the world to protect the oceans. That way the Indian Ocean and all of the oceans can remain a source of food, travel, and recreations for future generations.

Chapter Notes

Chapter 1. A Giant M
1. *The World Factbook 2002* (Washington, D.C.: Brassey's, 2002), p. 236.
2. Ibid.
3. Ibid.

Chapter 2. Resources From the Indian Ocean
1. Ray Sumner, *World Geography* (Hackensack, N.J.: Salem Press, Inc., 2001), p. 329.
2. Richard Ellis, *Encyclopedia of the Sea* (New York: Alfred A. Knopf, 2000), p. 164.
3. Lowell Field, "Persian Gulf Oil and Gas Exports Fact Sheet," *Energy Information Administration*, April 2003, <http://www.eia.doe.gov/cabs/pgulf.html> (December 8, 2003).
4. Ibid., pp. 1–3.
5. Trevor Day, *Oceans* (New York: Facts On File, Inc., 1999), p. 10.
6. Mary Emanoil, ed., *Encyclopedia of Endangered Species, Volume II* (Detroit: Gale Research Inc., 1994), p. 748.

Chapter 3. The Ocean Floor
1. Borgna Bruner, editor in chief, *Time Almanac 2003* (Boston, Mass.: Information Please, 2002).
2. Ray Sumner, *World Geography* (Hackensack, N.J.: Salem Press, Inc., 2001), p. 329.
3. Tom S. Garrison, *Essentials of Oceanography* (Pacific Grove, Calif.: Brooks/Cole, 2001), p. 46.
4. Richard Ellis, *Encyclopedia of the Sea* (New York: Alfred A. Knopf, 2000), p. 181.

Chapter 4. Life in the Indian Ocean
1. Mary Emanoil, ed., *Encyclopedia of Endangered Species, Volume II* (Detroit: Gale Research Inc., 1994), p. 137.
2. Tom S. Garrison, *Essentials of Oceanography* (Pacific Grove, Calif.: Brooks/Cole, 2001), p. 256.
3. Sally Morgan and Pauline Lalor, *Oceanlife* (London: PRC Publishing Ltd., 2001), p. 222.

Chapter 5. Exploration

1. Ray Sumner, *World Geography* (Hackensack, N.J.: Salem Press, Inc., 2001), p. 329.

2. Harold V. Thurman and Alan P. Trujillo, *Essentials of Oceanography* (New Jersey: Prentice Hall, 2002), p. 13.

3. Margaret Deacon, Tony Rice, and Colin Summerhayes, *Understanding the Oceans: A Century of Ocean Exploration* (New York: UCL Press, 2001), p. 15.

4. Ellen Prager, *The Oceans* (New York: McGraw-Hill, 2000), p. 147.

5. Tom S. Garrison, *Essentials of Oceanography* (Pacific Grove, Calif.: Brooks/Cole, 2001), p. 96.

6. Thurman and Trujillo, p. 98.

7. Prager, p. 189.

Chapter 6. A Healthy Ocean

1. Robert Simmon, "Oceanography from the Space Shuttle," *Goddard Space Flight Center*, August 1996, <http://daac.gsfc.nasa.gov/CAMPAIGN_DOCS/OCDST/shuttle_oceanography_web/oss_cover.html> (December 8, 2003).

2. Sylvia A. Earle, *Sea Change: A Message of the Oceans* (New York: G. P. Putnam's Sons, 1995), p. 274.

3. Ibid., p. 277.

4. Sally Morgan and Pauline Lalor, *Oceanlife* (London: PRC Publishing Ltd., 2001), p. 454.

5. Trevor Day, *Oceans* (New York: Facts On File, Inc., 1999), p. 10.

6. Stephen C. Jameson, et. al., "Regional Perspectives: Indian Ocean," Seas of the Middle East, May 1995, <http://www.ogp.noaa.gov/mpe/paleo/coral/sor/sor_indian.html> (December 8, 2003).

7. Mary Emanoil, ed., *Encyclopedia of Endangered Species, Volume II* (Detroit: Gale Research Inc.,1994), p. 833.

Further Reading

Aretha, David. *Discovering Asia's Land, People, and Wildlife.* Berkeley Heights, N.J.: MyReportLinks.com Books, 2004.

Goodman, Joan Elizabeth. *A Long and Uncertain Journey: The 27,000 Mile Voyage of Vasco da Gama.* New York: Mikaya Press, 2001.

Gray, Susan H. *Coral Reefs.* Minneapolis: Compass Point Books, 2001.

Lambert, David. *The Mediterranean Sea.* Austin, Tex.: Raintree Steck-Vaughn, 1997.

NgCheong-Lum, Roseline. *Maldives.* Tarrytown, N.Y.: Marshall Cavendish, 2003.

Penny, Malcolm. *The Indian Ocean.* Austin, Tex.: Raintree Steck-Vaughn, 1997.

Prevost, John F. *Indian Ocean.* Minneapolis: Abdo Publishing Company, 2003.

Sheppard, Charles. *Coral Reefs: Threats and Conservation.* Stillwater, Minn.: Voyageur Press, 2002.

Sonntag, Linda, and Trevor Norton. *The Atlas of the Oceans.* Brookfield, Conn.: Copper Beech Books, 2001.

Taylor, Leighton. *The Indian Ocean.* Farmington Hills, Mich.: Gale Group, 1998.

Vieira, Linda. *The Seven Seas: Exploring the World Ocean.* New York: Walker & Company, 2003.

Waterlow, Julia. *The Red Sea and the Arabian Gulf.* Austin, Tex.: Raintree Steck-Vaughn, 1997.

Ylvisaker, Anne. *The Indian Ocean.* Mankato, Minn.: Bridgestone Books, 2003.